De[illegible]

Danger

by Meish Goldish

illustrated by Diana Kizlauskas

Harcourt
SCHOOL PUBLISHERS

Printed in the United States of America

ISBN 10: 0-15-351119-2
ISBN 13: 978-0-15-351119-6

Ordering Options
ISBN 10: 0-15-350603-2 (Grade 6 On-Level Collection)
ISBN 13: 978-0-15-350603-1 (Grade 6 On-Level Collection)
ISBN 10: 0-15-357989-7 (package of 5)
ISBN 13: 978-0-15-357989-9 (package of 5)

2 3 4 5 6 7 8 9 10   179   12 11 10 09 08 07

Jodi gazed out the car window as her family drove across southeast California. They were traveling through the Mojave Desert. Jodi had never seen the desert before, although she had heard much about it from her parents. They had visited the Mojave Desert once before she was born. Now they wanted to share the same experience with her.

Jodi was happy to be in the desert. Over the years, she had enjoyed seeing the colorful photos that her parents had taken during their first trip to the Mojave. Jodi loved to take pictures. She had brought her camera along for the trip. As the car moved forward, she snapped photos of cactus plants and wildflowers that grew on the side of the road. She hoped to get some shots of jackrabbits and lizards in the area.

Suddenly, the car slowed, jerked for a moment, and stopped. "Are we getting out here?" Jodi asked.

Dad shook his head. "I hadn't planned on it," he sighed, "but the car seems to have broken down. We've got enough gas, so I know that's not the problem. It must be something else. I'll check it out."

Dad got out of the car and lifted the front hood. He gazed at the engine and winced. Steam seemed to be rising everywhere. "Looks like we've got engine trouble," he announced. "Everybody out of the car."

Jodi and her mother exited the car. Dad said, "Why don't you two walk around a little and enjoy the desert scenery while I fiddle with the engine. I may be able to fix it shortly."

Jodi and her mother began to explore the area. Jodi snapped several photos of the cactus plants nearby. "Do you know what kind of cactus that is?" Jodi asked, approaching the spiky plant gingerly.

Mom smiled and replied, “It’s called a barrel cactus because it’s shaped like a barrel. Do you see all those tough, curved spines on the outside of the plant? Long ago, Native Americans used them as fishhooks.”

“Wow, Mom, you sure know a lot about *cactuses!*” Jodi exclaimed.

Mom laughed and said, “Well, I don’t want to sound cocky, but I’ve learned quite a lot about plants over the years. By the way, when you talk about more than one cactus, most people say *cacti.*”

“I hope Dad has learned as much about car engines as you have about *cacti,*” Jodi joked. “It’s getting really hot out here.”

Jodi and her mother continued to walk. Jodi snapped some close-ups of the cacti with her camera. "I don't understand how these plants can survive in such hot weather," she said.

Mom smiled and replied, "It is an amazing thing, isn't it? The desert temperature rises well over a hundred degrees during the day. Out here, there's not much rainfall, either. However, the barrel cactus is prepared when it does rain. Its stems store water so that the plant doesn't die."

Jodi looked puzzled. "What keeps animals around here from eating the plants?" she asked.

Mom patted Jodi on the shoulders. She then pointed to the cactus. "Remember how I told you these sharp spines were once used as fishhooks?" she asked. "Well, those same spines also prevent animals from eating the cactus."

Mom wiped her brow and said, “It really is getting hot. Let’s see how your father is doing with the engine.”

The two walked back to the car. Dad didn’t look very hopeful. “I can’t seem to get the engine working,” he sighed. “This heat is really starting to get to me, too. I’m afraid we’ll have to call for help.”

Mom took out the cell phone from her purse. “I can’t seem to get a good signal from here—that means I can’t dial for help.”

Dad sighed. “Even though we have a cell phone, we’re stymied because we have no signal!”

Jodi and her parents sat inside the car again. "What do we do now?" Jodi asked.

Dad looked at his watch. "It'll be getting dark in a couple of hours," he said. "Let's hope someone comes along before then. I'll ask whoever drives by to drive into town and call an acquaintance of mine who lives not too far from here. He'll be able to help us."

"What if no one comes by?" Jodi asked nervously. "We seem to be pretty far off the main road."

Dad smiled and said, "Don't worry, sweetie, someone will find us soon."

The three of them sat in the car for a long time. For a while, Mom and Dad talked about their first trip to the desert. Jodi had a hard time enjoying the conversation.

"I'm really thirsty," she announced.

Mom took out a bottle of water, and the three of them shared it, but they were still thirsty after draining the contents.

Mom said, "Fortunately, we do have that other big jug of water in the car. We should save it, though, in case we're stuck out here for a long time." Dad nodded his head in agreement.

The desert sun continued to beat down on the car. The car seats grew hotter and hotter. "This heat is unbearable," Jodi exclaimed.

“I have an idea,” Dad said. He got out of the car, walked to the back, and opened the trunk. Jodi watched as he retrieved several blankets.

“Why does Dad want blankets?” Jodi asked Mom. “We’re too hot, not too cold.”

Jodi watched as Dad took the blankets and walked over to two cacti of even height. He draped one of the blankets between two cacti, creating some shade. He folded the other one neatly between the two cacti on the desert floor. Then he explained, “This blanket will shield out some of the sunlight. That should keep us a little cooler. This blanket on the ground will make us a little more comfortable.”

The three continued to sit and look for any passing cars, but none came. Meanwhile, Jodi's stomach began to rumble, even as her thirst grew. "Mom, Dad, do we still have turkey sandwiches in the car? I know we were saving them for dinner, but may I have one now?"

Mom smiled and shook her head. "The human body needs extra water to digest food, so eating will actually make you feel thirstier. Remember the cactus? It has special adaptations to keep it from getting thirsty. We humans don't have those adaptations, so instead, we have to adapt our behavior. Let's just stay still and cool in the shade until it gets dark."

Jodi thought for a moment. "Speaking of the cactus," she said, "I read somewhere that you can eat cactus pulp, and it will quench your thirst. Can't we just cut open the cactus?"

"That may be tempting," said Dad, "but there are several reasons we can't do that. First of all, cacti aren't really juicy at all times of the year. The flesh would probably be very fibrous and tough. Secondly, most cacti are mildly poisonous. Even if you did get juice from the pulp, it would make you very sick, and that would dehydrate you even more. Third, cutting the top off of a cactus kills the whole plant, and is illegal in most states."

"Not to mention that even non-poisonous cactus flesh tastes absolutely rank," said Mom, laughing.

Jodi nodded in understanding. “Ok, then, let’s tell stories to pass the time. That way we can stay still and conserve our water until the sun goes down.”

As the hours went by, Jodi and her parents no longer noticed their thirst. They knew everything would be all right. Someone would come along to help them eventually. However, the sun was now setting, and the evening air had turned cold.

“Before it was so hot,” Jodi remarked, “and now it’s cold. Is the desert always like this?”

“Yes,” Mom replied, smiling. “The temperature goes from one extreme to the other. Let’s get back in the car now. It will be warmer in there.”

Jodi and her parents retrieved the blankets from the cacti and headed to their automobile. Dad brought the blankets inside and handed them to Mom and Jodi.

"This is our motel for tonight," Dad joked, "so bundle up warmly."

Jodi stretched out on the back seat and tried to relax. All was quiet for a few minutes. Suddenly, she heard a howling outside. "What's that?" she asked.

"Just a coyote," Dad explained. "Most of the desert animals come out at night, when it's cooler. Don't be surprised if you see a few jackrabbits hopping around the car. There might even be a fox or two, so make sure your doors stay locked."

Jodi buried herself under the blanket and was soon sound asleep.

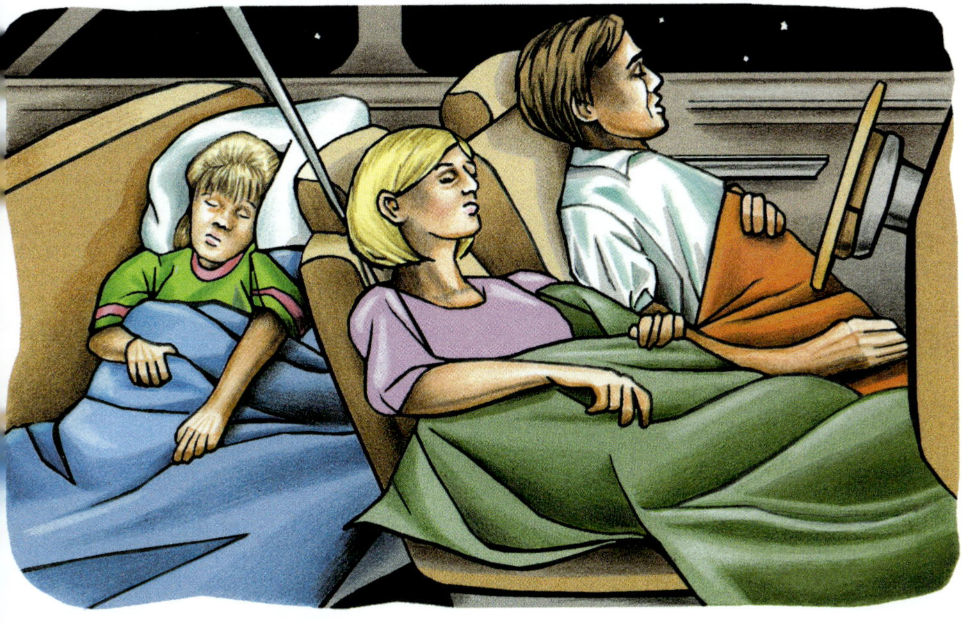

Early the next morning, Jodi and her parents were awakened by a knock on the car window. A police officer stood outside. Dad rolled down his window.

"Are you okay?" the officer asked.

"Yes," Dad replied, "but our car engine may have a terminal problem, and our cell phone would not work out here."

"I can get you some help right away," the officer said.

Jodi peered out the window and grew very excited. "Look!" she exclaimed. "Look at all the animals!" She grabbed her camera and quickly began to take photos of the jackrabbits, lizards, and kangaroo rats that scampered near the car. "This is amazing!" she cried.

"I guess this visit won't keep you from coming back to the Mojave, will it?" Mom said, smiling.

"Are you kidding?" Jodi cried. "I want to visit the Mojave every year! I'm like a cactus. I've learned how to survive here!"

Think Critically

1 Why was Jodi puzzled that a cactus could survive in the desert?

2 What made Jodi feel uncomfortable in the desert?

3 How did Jodi's family manage to survive in the Mojave?

4 Were you surprised that Jodi ended up liking the desert? Explain.

5 What important lesson about life did Jodi's experience teach her?

Science

Map With your class, research where deserts in the United States are located. Draw a map of the United States. Color and label deserts on the map.

School-Home Connection Tell your family the story of Jodi and her parents. Explain how the desert turned from hot to cold. Discuss whether you would rather live in a place that is always hot or always cold. Give reasons to support your choice.

Word Count: 1,607